S0-AGT-718

OUR COMPANY

In 1928, at the age of twenty-two, Peter Beilenson began printing books on a small press in the basement of his parents' home in Larchmont, New York. Peter—and later, his wife, Edna—sought to create fine books that sold at "prices even a pauper could afford."

Today, still family owned and operated, Peter Pauper Press continues to honor our founders' legacy of quality, value, and fun for big kids and small kids alike.

For my son, William Wolf

Images used under license from Shutterstock.com

Designed by Heather Zschock and Margaret Rubiano

Visit us at peterpauper.com

LET'S MAKE A MOViE!

CONTENTS

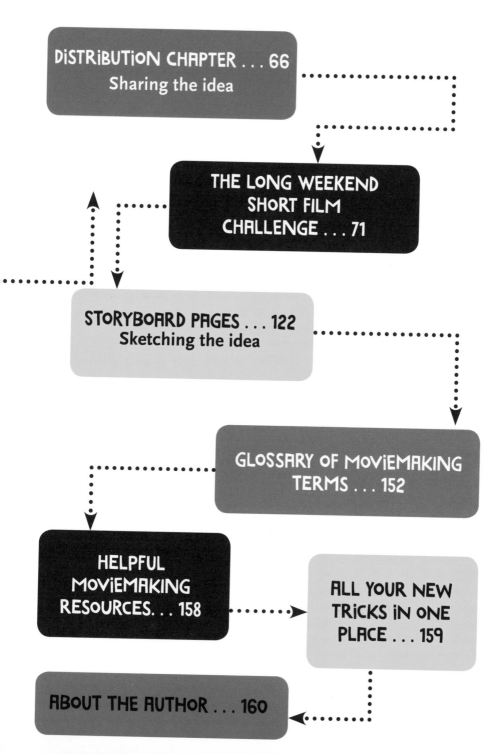

INTRODUCTION

FREEZE RIGHT WHERE YOU ARE.

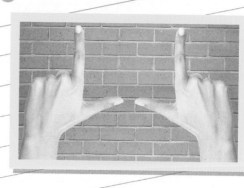

- Make two L shapes with your hands and then hold them together, thumbs touching each other. This is your frame.

- Now hold this finger-frame about one foot from your face and close one eye. **What do you see?**

- Slowly move this frame around your room and find something interesting. A T-shirt slung over a chair, a toy mostly hidden by your bed, a splash of sunlight on the wall.

- Hold your finger-frame over your subject and hum a little song.

- Now slowly move your finger-frame away from your face to zoom in. The frame will get tighter around your subject. OR slowly pull your fingers closer to your eyes to zoom out.

- There! You just started dreaming up the first **shot** of your movie. Capture that first shot with a phone or tablet and save it for later.

Welcome to Let's Make a Movie!, the supercharged interactive guide to turning your amazing ideas into awesome movies! My name is Danny and I love movies. I've made movies and the music in movies for years! And since we live in The Future, or will be by the time you're reading this, I'm pleased to say there is nothing that can stop you from using your amazing ideas to make movies of your own.

BUT FIRST, WHAT IS A MOVIE?

Dictionaries say a movie is an event or a story "recorded with a camera." That is a simple but PERFECT definition for us, because this book will focus on using movies to tell stories.

Stories come in all sizes. They are short clips of your life, epic invented journeys, and everything in between.

We humans used images to tell stories long before we used words to tell stories. Example: Cave drawings found in early human settlements! These drawings include pictures of animals, which are the cast of characters, and pictures of humans, which are pretty much the credits at the end. These drawings shared the stories of the day.

Add the flickering fire within the cave and I'll bet that was one scary wildebeest stampede!

"Once upon a time I ran away from these stampeding beasts and lived to tell the story!"

Now we live in a magical time of pocket computers otherwise known as The Future, and it has never been easier to share ideas and stories as movies. Snapchat, Instagram, and Musical.ly let millions of people upload tiny stories every day. YouTube and Vimeo have more than 500 hours of video uploaded every minute.

So—in a world where you can always watch something new, why should YOU make a movie?

Because **NO ONE HAS YOUR IDEAS!**
And if you choose to share them, they will be original and amazing because they are yours! The world from your perspective is a whole new world. But hey, that's just *my* reason why you should make a movie. Now you need to come up with a reason of your own.

Why do you need a reason? You don't always. But most of the time a reason will help you focus the story you're telling. Go back to our cave artists. If their reason for a story was to warn others about a scary beast, they would draw or paint its image (like the picture to the right). The artist's reason for painting the picture influences the way they create the picture.

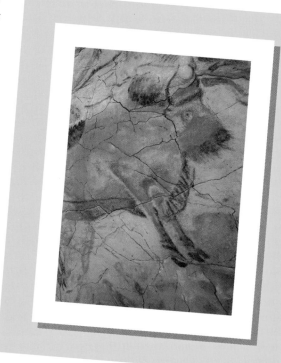

Here's a list of possible reasons for you to make a movie. Pick one or come up with some on your own and add them to the list.

POSSIBLE LIST OF REASONS TO MAKE A MOVIE:

★ TO SHARE YOUR TRUTH

★ TO SAVE AN IDEA FOR LATER

★ TO CELEBRATE A FRIEND OR FAMILY MEMBER

★ TO POINT OUT SOMETHING RIDICULOUS

★ TO SCARE

★ TO DELIGHT

★ TO INSPIRE

★ TO FILL AN OTHERWISE OPEN WEEKEND

★ ....

★ ....

★ ....

Have you picked one? GREAT!

Now that you have your reason, let's make a movie!

NOTE: The moviemaking terms in this book that are in red bold type are further explained in the Glossary at the back.

INSPIRATION CHAPTER

DREAMING UP THE IDEA

LET'S MAKE THAT MOVIE! BUT WHAT KIND?

★ Are you one of those **freaky types** who wants to scare everybody with a gory horror film?

★ Are you one of those **silly types** who wants to make a laugh-out-loud comedy movie?

★ Are you one of those **romantic types** who wants to film a powerful "Goodbye" in the rain?

Person 1: "You said you were leaving and never coming back."

Person 2: "Well, I, um, forgot my umbrella."

No matter what kind of movie you want to make, it's a process. There are many little goals to accomplish before you can say, "That's a wrap."

"That's a wrap" is a filmmaking phrase people say when they are finished with a movie. (By the way, we'll point out other filmmaking words and phrases throughout the book and put them in the Glossary in the back. Your new moviemaking vocabulary will be in one place!)

Making a movie is a big undertaking. This book will show you a proven process, but at the end of the day:

TRICK #1: GO YOUR OWN WAY!

I don't mean go away! Stay! Keep this book open! Yikes, that was close.

This book will show (and follow) the process most filmmakers use when they make movies. This is the process followed by big movie studios, small independent filmmakers, and everyone in between. We'll talk about what makes a good story and how to write it, then how to film it, finish it, and share it.

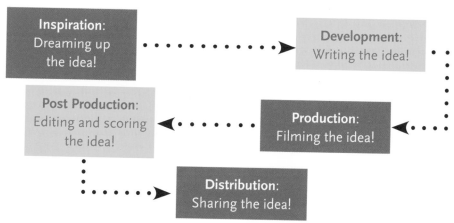

Inspiration: Dreaming up the idea!

Development: Writing the idea!

Post Production: Editing and scoring the idea!

Production: Filming the idea!

Distribution: Sharing the idea!

Each step takes different skills to complete. It's like doing a bunch of jobs to create one awesome final product. In this book, we call those jobs "wearing different hats." You might wear a Writing Hat, Directing Hat, Acting Hat, and/or an Editing Hat. Or you might be making a movie with friends, which means they'll wear some of those hats. No matter what hat you're wearing, knowing this order will help organize your process. Bonus: You will sound SUPER professional when you talk about your movie to adults!

At any point, if you decide you have found a different way to make a movie, don't wait. Just flip to the blank pages in this book and start writing! Or maybe set this book aside, grab a camera, and start filming! All these tricks and tips will still be waiting for you when you get back. Speaking of tricks, there is one trick that is most important, and that is:

TRICK #2:   SAVE YOUR IDEAS!

If you ask most adult directors, writers, and artists, they'll tell you they wish they had the imagination of a kid. Guess what, YOU DO! So right now, while your brain is a magical, mushy, growing glob of brilliant imagination, a limitless creative engine, a churning whirlpool of weird and wonderful thoughts, SAVE YOUR IDEAS! Even if you decide not to make a movie this weekend, this summer, or even this year, your incredible ideas will be waiting for you here when you come back.

That's what all the space here is for!

Well, *this* space above is being used for a llama rolling out pizza dough, but there is a ton of other space in the back of this journal.

Also in the back of this book: The Long Weekend Short Film Challenge with five different movie prompts that will challenge you to write, direct, edit, and share a movie in a single weekend! Are you up to the challenge of a mini-filmmaking process? If so, you can:

★ MAKE A COMEDY (page 72)

★ MAKE A GHOST STORY (page 82)

★ MAKE A DOCUMENTARY (page 92)

★ MAKE AN ACTION MOVIE (page 102)

★ MAKE A SUPERHERO MOVIE (page 112)

But let's talk about the regular filmmaking process first. So, grab that "List of Reasons to Make a Movie" from page 10!

DEVELOPMENT CHAPTER
CHAPTER

WRITING THE IDEA

Let's develop a story, write a script, build a team, get a **cast**, and otherwise set you up for success in making your movie. First, we'll need something to develop! This means we need to come up with a story that shows off all those ideas of yours. But before we start brainstorming, I have a trick:

TRICK #3: "GOOD WRITERS BORROW BUT GREAT WRITERS STEAL."

This quote has been credited to several famous artists, including Pablo Picasso and Igor Stravinsky. A person named W. H. Davenport Adams said it first in an article complaining about bad poets. What does it mean? What's the difference between borrowing and stealing? Here's what I think:

When you *borrow* an idea, you must say where you got it from so that it stays that other person's idea. You give them credit and, in some cases, pay them. However, when you *steal* an idea, you must be cunning and artful. You can only take a precious little part, or parts—the parts that matter most to you. Then, when you sit down to write them, you must change the parts to make them fit their new purpose.

The process of twisting and modifying a "stolen" bit of an idea transforms it into a new idea! Then it's yours and someone else can sneakily "steal" it from you. Maybe it's more truthful to say, "Good writers borrow and great writers are inspired by other people's work," but I think "steal" sounds better.

Why am I starting this chapter with a trick about being sneaky? Because . . .

TRICK #4:   THERE ARE NO NEW STORIES, JUST NEW TELLINGS.

People love to say the first half of this trick to each other when they have **writer's block** or are otherwise feeling uncreative. I get it. Feeling unoriginal can be hard. It can make a blank page seem a lot bigger than it really is. **If you feel stuck, try playing the "Flip Game"—telling an old story in a wacky new way.**

Here is a list of stories I flipped. Start brainstorming your own flippable ideas. Even if you don't write these stories, thinking about them can help get your creativity flowing.

FLIPPABLE STORIES:

* ★ ***Cinderella*** as told from the pumpkin's perspective.

* ★ ***Peter Pan*** as told by a random English fellow who saw all the flying children.

* ★ An alien who eats people because it thinks each one is a pineapple and is SO upset when they are not!

* ★ The horses who don't love that their knights wear all that very heavy armor.

* ★ A rock that ends up getting placed in an ugly stone wall.

"No no no no no . . . oh, shoot."

Now that you're not feeling stuck, let's start from scratch.

There are lots of ways to write a story. Sometimes a story happens to you or comes in a dream and all you need to do is write it down as a **script**, which is what people call a story written as *Who said What Where*. The rest of the time (most of the time), writing a story and turning it into a script can be lots of work. Start by trying to describe your story as simply as you can. For instance:

My story is about: A _____ character being changed

by a _____ in a _____.

Use the spaces to fill in the details of your story. Play with the wording but this very basic description should reveal that a character is changed by an event that takes place in their story world. Here are two examples:

If you were writing a fighting space epic you might say:

A <u>secretly magical</u> character is changed by a <u>war among the stars that arrives unexpectedly</u> on <u>his desert planet.</u>

About magical characters

Of course, your character does not need to be secretly magical . . . but it's a creative choice people love to use because the audience gets to learn something huge about the main character at the same time the character gets to learn it about themselves.

If you were writing an educationally-themed magic **franchise** movie you might say:

A <u>secretly magical</u> character is changed by <u>seven years of classes</u> in an <u>incredibly dangerous school for wizards.</u>

Use this fill-in-the-blank way to get started on your story, then leave it behind as your story grows and becomes WAY too complicated for just one sentence. Then, when you're finished, go back and see if you'd still write the same sentence. If things have changed, write a new one.

Here are some blanks for you to fill in!

A _____ character being changed by a

_____ in a _____.

A _____ character being changed by a

_____ in a _____.

A _____ character being changed by a

_____ in a _____.

PRODUCTION _____

DIRECTOR _____

CAMERA _____

DATE   SCENE   TAKE

Now that you have this one great sentence describing the story you want to tell, let's figure out the best way to tell it.

We're gonna break the story up into three **acts**. The word "acts" just means "parts." Why do we break up a movie into acts? Giving the story three acts, or parts—the Beginning, the Middle, and the End—will help you organize the action so that it builds, getting more intense as you go.

Here is an example of a comedy in a **three-act structure**:

ACT 1: BEGINNING

★ Meet the main character and learn what makes them sort of weird. (Maybe meet their friend, or friends.)

★ Discover the main character's big problem.

ACT 2: MIDDLE

★ The main character tries to solve their problem *and fails*!

★ The character tries to solve the problem *again* and fails!

★ The character tries something new and weird to solve their problem and . . .

ACT 3: END

★ . . . THEY DON'T FAIL!

★ There is celebrating, exciting music, and sometimes even kissing.

When you start writing your movie, you'll find that each of the three acts has different challenges. Following are a few tricks to get you (and your main character!) through each act. **An extra hint: Each act should tell a small story in itself.**

TRICK #5:   ACT 1 — MAKE YOUR HERO SOMEONE WE ROOT FOR.

This might seem obvious, but if you think about different characters in movies, maybe it's not. If you've ever started watching a movie, but didn't feel like finishing it, chances are it's because the person who made the movie didn't know this trick. Learn from their mistake and make your **hero** someone (or something) likable! The more likable they are, the more the audience will care about them solving their problem. Here is a list of some likable qualities:

★ Keeps their room amazingly clean.

★ Takes care of stray animals.

★ Shares the loaf of bread they just bought with two hungry kids.

★ Remains super positive about life despite some personal difficulty.

But . . . sometimes a hero is an **anti-hero**—they're also the bad gal or bad guy. This is extra tricky because an audience hopes they succeed and hopes that they fail at the same time!

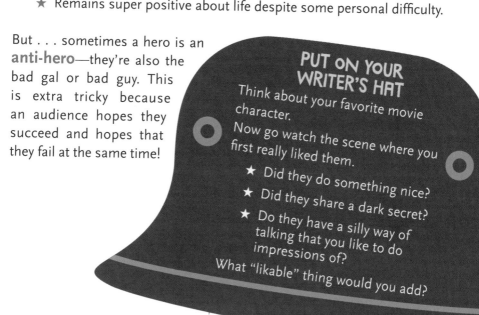

PUT ON YOUR WRITER'S HAT

Think about your favorite movie character.

Now go watch the scene where you first really liked them.

★ Did they do something nice?

★ Did they share a dark secret?

★ Do they have a silly way of talking that you like to do impressions of?

What "likable" thing would you add?

Now that you know who your character is and why they're so interesting to watch, let's make things hard for them with a little trick called:

TRICK #6: ACT 2 — ONE LOCK AND THREE BAD KEYS

Come up with one Big Problem for your main character to solve. Then let him or her have at least three attempts to solve it that DO NOT work. Think: How lame it would be if in a superhero movie, the **villain's** plan was ruined on the first try? NO! We want to see your likable hero struggle and fail as long as we can. Give them hints, and help, and tiny victories along the way, but DON'T let them win until you absolutely have to. Example:

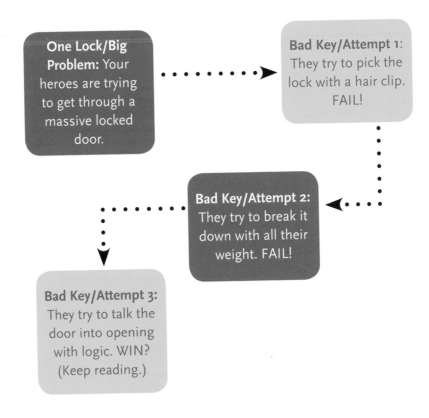

TRICK #7:   ACT 3 — TOO MUCH OF A GOOD THING

Humans are fickle, which means they rarely know what they really want, and that is true even when they get it. A trick for your third act is to give your character what they first wanted, but *what they thought they wanted* gets to be TOO MUCH, and they realize it's something they didn't actually want at all.

Like ice cream!

Let's say we're writing a story about a guy named Todd. Todd is our hero. He's super likable because we watched him save a caterpillar from being squished, so we're rooting for him. Todd's favorite thing in the whole world is strawberry ice cream. Todd's gonna spend our whole movie trying to find that creamy strawberry goodness!

★ First, Todd goes looking for an ice cream parlor. But they're all closed. FAIL!

★ Then he tries to buy strawberry ice cream at the supermarket. But he has no money. FAIL!

★ Then Todd decides to make strawberry ice cream himself. WIN, right?

Wrong! Todd misreads the recipe and accidentally makes a zillion gallons of strawberry ice cream! It fills his entire kitchen, and he has to spend the day eating his way out. *That* is too much of a good thing!

What's the difference between a good story and a great story?

One of the differences has to do with exceeding expectations. In the case of movies, this means surprising the audience with something they didn't think was coming. The surprise doesn't need to jump out of the dark and terrify them. The surprise can be the believability of an acting performance, the rich details of an invented world, or a clever twist. So, when you think you've got a good story, STOP, go back, and look through it for one or two things you can upgrade from normal to amazing. A good trick for this is...

TRICK #8:   **SEE THE MOVIE BEFORE YOU MAKE THE MOVIE.**

Some writers and directors are especially good at this. When you look inside their personal journals, there are pages of scribbled lines of **dialogue** and sketches of camera shots that are exactly like the final product.

But seeing the final product from the beginning is HARD. It's a skill in itself, like rope-skipping or calligraphy. But it's also helpful for honing in on things that can be improved. Therefore, one way to picture your **"picture"** is to write or draw it out by hand.

Oh, wait. I forgot to ask . . .

. . . Are you ready to wear the **Director**'s Hat? People spend years preparing for this most important of tasks. It takes vision and decisive action to transform a story from page to screen. Let's exercise that vision with a **storyboard**. Storyboards are basically comics—comics that show what will happen in each shot and how a camera can capture the best version of it.

Let's storyboard some of Todd's ice cream story, which we could call **Straw-Buried!** (Except that that would give away the ending.) Here are a few examples with some of the camera terms directors use in storyboards.

Push in on an ice cream-deprived Todd.

Squared off camera as Todd goes running through the **frame**.

Close up on his empty wallet.

Pull out to see how big the ice cream mixing bowl is.

Wide shot of Todd's kitchen, with ice cream ingredients everywhere.

Even the wildest, most super-charged story needs something *true* in it, something that makes the audience connect personally with the character or characters on the screen. We may have never met a Wookiee from *Star Wars* before, but we can all relate to having a friend only you understand. The fastest way to find something true for your own story is:

TRICK #9: START WITH WHAT IS TRUE FOR YOU!

You are the best judge of what is true for you. And the more you base your character's wants and wishes on the things you believe, the more believable your character will be. You may think your script can't have many of your truths because it is set in space, in a volcano, or has only animal characters. But I challenge you to find some small part of yourself to tuck inside your story.

TRICK #10: WRITE IT RIGHT.

This is the first trick that feels a little like a "rule." A script is also called a **screenplay**, and has a very specific format. Screenplays use special abbreviations and codes to make writing and filming easier (and learning how to write scripts harder).

There are some great screenwriting resources online that can help you format correctly, such as **WriterDuet** (writerduet.com), **DubScript** (dubscript.com), and **Plotbot** (plotbot.com), and they offer free and paid "pro" versions. You just need an email address and someone to download it for you. If you tell them you read about the programs here, they'll give you a student discount for the pro version.

Correct screenplay formatting will help the people you are working with see your movie in their heads while they're reading it. However, unless you're trying to sell your screenplay to a big studio, you can write it "wrong" for now or write it sort of right for now because at the end of the day, the most important thing is that your script includes all the amazing ideas you have for your story, your audience, and your **actors**.

Speaking of actors,

Actors are great! They bring
your words to life. Sometimes they'll show up and know exactly how they
want to act. Sometimes they'll show up ready to figure it out with you.

Being an actor is hard. They pretend to be real, while they pretend they aren't pretending, all while pretending there isn't a camera there capturing them pretending not to pretend! If you are making a movie with actors, you might start by holding **auditions**. Copy the page below and use it to make notes when you pick the actors for your movie.

Actor Audition Exercise

Write down the actor's name and contact information.

Have each actor say their name and the part they are there for.

Ask them a few normal questions to make them feel comfortable:

★ "How are you?"

★ "What's your spirit animal?"

★ "Do you have a favorite breakfast food?"

Have them act a short section of your script. They don't need to memorize it. (These short sections are called **sides**.)

To get an idea of what it's like to work with each actor, give them a bit of direction on their acting. And have them act out the scene again. Here are some things you might say:

★ "Try it again but this time, try not to smile."

★ "Try it again but this time, try shouting at the end."

★ "Try it again but this time, imagine your character is three kids wearing a trench coat standing on each other's shoulders."

Make notes about each actor and their performance.

When you're choosing your actors, don't just pick the most popular or most famous person you know. Find actors who are easy and fun to work with, who make you excited about your movie. To help you find the right actors, it might be helpful to think about them as **collaborators**, other people with good ideas who can make your story even better.

A note about collaborators

When you work with a good collaborator, every idea you have gets better. And it doesn't feel like you are adding ideas together, it feels like you are *multiplying* ideas together. Suddenly you realize you haven't come up with just two cool ideas, you've come up with *four,* then *eight,* then *forty!*

As the director, you will be making a lot of decisions quickly. Here's a trick to get you ready:

TRICK #11:   **EVERY IDEA IS YOUR BEST IDEA . . .
UNTIL THE NEXT IDEA!**

You can absolutely handle your role as director. How do I know? Look at where you are. You're on page 33 of a book about making movies. You're motivated! Intelligent! Ready! So, take a deep breath and believe in yourself. Being a director is about having confidence in your ideas—so much confidence that you won't be afraid to change an idea when a better one comes along.

PUT ON YOUR DiRECTOR'S HAT

Imagine *re-casting* one of your own favorite films with different actors. Can you imagine someone who you think would be better as a certain character? Can you imagine someone who would be much worse?

Casting is just one decision a director makes (in big productions the director often has the help of a **Casting Director**, too), but it's certainly one audiences remember.

And guess what? Everything changes once you walk out onto your set with your actors, your script, and your ideas. Next we come to . . .

PRODUCTION CHAPTER

FILMING THE IDEA

Let's organize **the shoot**, film the action, eat some snacks, and otherwise have a great production to set you up for success in the **editing** process. You already have your script, your actors, and your ideas.

Being on a set can be crazy. There are lots of different jobs and, depending on the size of your **crew**, there are lots of different people doing those jobs. If it's just you, that's fine, too. Plenty of people make their first movie wearing multiple hats at once. And if that's you this time, I have a trick for you:

"More concealer!"
Makeup Artist:
Makes sure the actors' faces look great.

"I need last looks!"
Costumer: Makes sure the actors' clothes look great.

"I need room tone!"
Sound Editor:
Makes sure the movie sounds great.

"I need a new zombie catch phrase."
Writer:
Revises the script on set.

"Scene 2, take 4."
Production Assistant:
Assists the production.

"I need this wonderful crew!"
Executive Producer:
Puts the team together that makes the movie happen.

KNOW WHAT HAT YOU'RE WEARING.

In normal life, it's fine to switch "hats" for each task or activity. For instance, you might wear a "School Hat," a "Sports Team Hat," or a "Big Sister [or] Brother Hat." On a movie set, because all the jobs are so specific, you need to be clear about what job you're doing at each moment. One way to do that is to picture switching between jobs with actual hats.

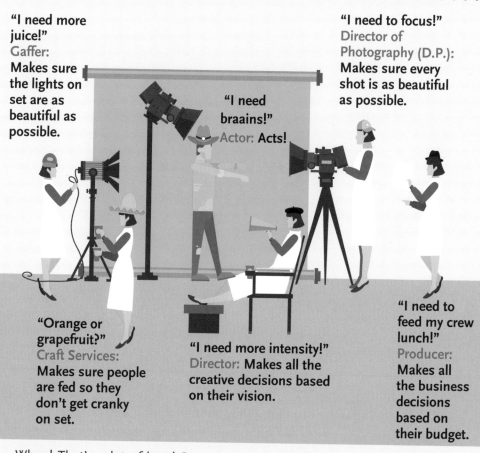

"I need more juice!"
Gaffer: Makes sure the lights on set are as beautiful as possible.

"I need braains!"
Actor: Acts!

"I need to focus!"
Director of Photography (D.P.): Makes sure every shot is as beautiful as possible.

"Orange or grapefruit?"
Craft Services: Makes sure people are fed so they don't get cranky on set.

"I need more intensity!"
Director: Makes all the creative decisions based on their vision.

"I need to feed my crew lunch!"
Producer: Makes all the business decisions based on their budget.

Whoa! That's a lot of hats! So, you may decide that bringing a few other people along on this adventure is a good idea. Two heads are better than one when it comes to wearing all those hats.

MOVIES ARE A GREAT TEAM SPORT.

A filmmaker often works alone in coming up with a movie story and ideas. But once you're on set, it's a sprint in every direction to a thousand different finish lines! Having a group of people around to support your good decisions (and gently question your bad ones) can be super helpful. A movie is like a team sport, where different positions do different things. The following pages contain a list of moviemaking jobs. Check off each hat you've worn, as well as the date and the name of the film you made when you wore it. Check off the whole set and you'll have a better understanding of the moviemaking process than 90 percent of the people who go to see movies!

☐ **Actor**

....

....

....

☐ **Composer**

....

....

....

☐ **Costumer**

....

....

....

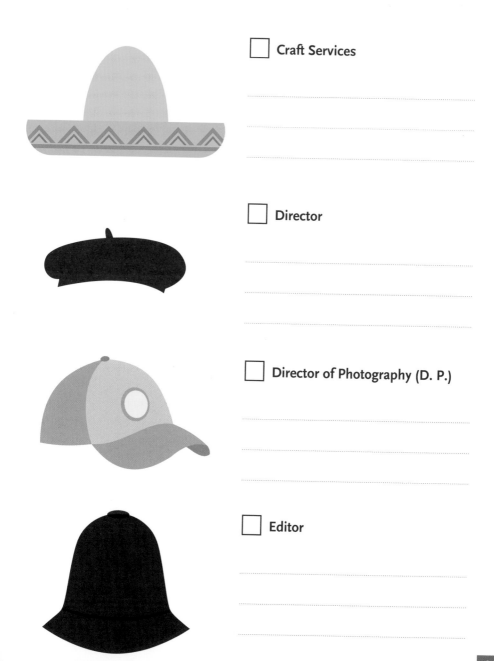

☐ Craft Services

....

....

☐ Director

....

....

☐ Director of Photography (D. P.)

....

....

....

☐ Editor

....

....

....

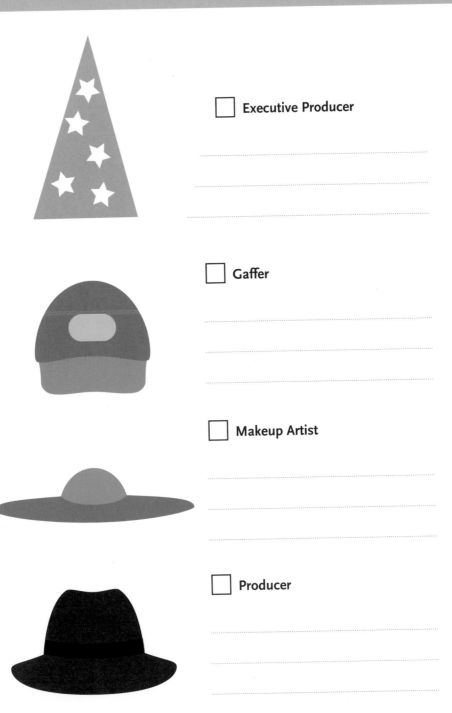

☐ **Executive Producer**

....

....

....

☐ **Gaffer**

....

....

....

☐ **Makeup Artist**

....

....

....

☐ **Producer**

....

....

....

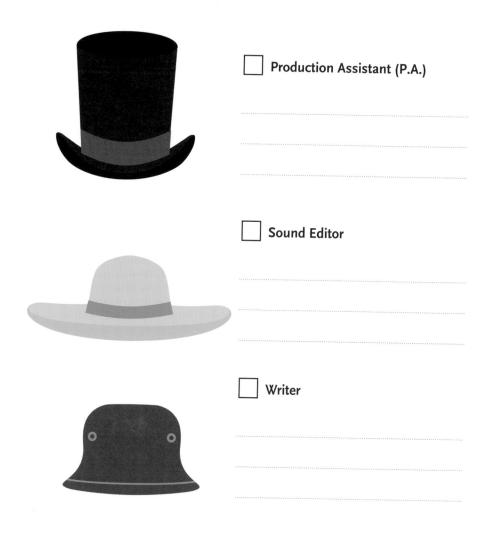

☐ **Production Assistant (P.A.)**

....
....
....

☐ **Sound Editor**

....
....
....

☐ **Writer**

....
....
....

Now that you have a crew and you're ready to start filming, it's time for the MOST USEFUL trick in this book! It's so important, I'm gonna show you.

TURN THAT PHONE!

Make your movies in landscape mode! Chances are you're using your phone or tablet camera for filming. The fastest way to make your movie better is to turn that device to a horizontal position and fill the camera frame. You can get a tripod to hold the camera still and lots of other gadgets to help you film, but nothing will do more than simply turning the phone to landscape.

**PUT ON YOUR
PRODUCTION ASSISTANT
(P.A.) HAT**

The next time you see a movie, try to count the number of names in the credits. Was it more than 100? More than 1,000? Are there jobs you've never heard about?

You may have already noticed: The back cover of this book has a picture of a **slate board** (also known as a **clapperboard**, **slapperboard**, **sound marker**, and other names). It's that thing the P.A. was holding on page 36. A slate board lets you write on it the scene you are filming and how many times you film it. If you want, you can buy a fancy slate board that snaps when you close it. The reason they snap is so an editor can sync the film to the sound later. You can also just slap the front of this book, or have someone clap their hands.

(Okay, you can make your book vertical again.)

When your phone is turned to landscape mode you can:

TRICK #15:   **SET THE SHOT.**

Let's take some time to figure out what *belongs in* your shot and what would be better *left out*. You can teach your audience a lot with every shot in your movie. Let me show you what I mean with this pineapple. Why a pineapple? It is a very photogenic fruit.

MID: This is a pretty normal shot. You might see this in a commercial for pineapples. You know what you are looking at, but it's kind of boring.

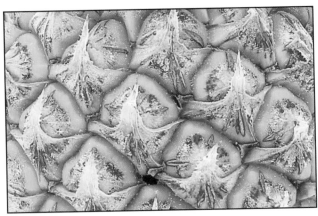

TIGHT: This close-up offers a thoughtful comment on the nature of tough outward appearances giving way to inner sweetness.

WIDE: Now that's a lonely pineapple!

See the range of information communicated just from the distance of your shot to your subject?

Now let's think about movement. For right now let's either move the camera or have your subject move. Let's switch from a pineapple to a car.

NO, not a pineapple car, a regular car.

I see those wheels!

Okay, fine!

Your car driving straight through a shot without stopping doesn't engage your audience. Instead it leaves them behind.

But if your camera stays on the car, the audience will feel like the story is headed somewhere.

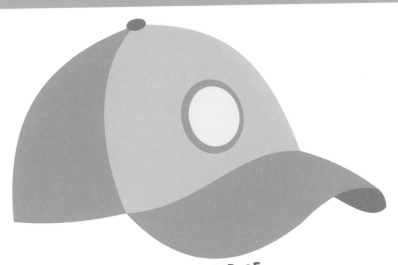

PUT ON YOUR DiRECTOR OF PHOTOGRAPHY (D.P.) HAT

Pick a movie you like and watch a scene right in the middle. But first, mute the sound. Watch the scene but only pay attention to what the camera is doing. (This is easier with a movie you've seen a bunch of times.) When does the camera shake? When does it follow the action? When is it still?

These are all big choices and they affect how you feel about what you are seeing.

Use the next storyboards to practice framing your shots as wide, mid, or tight, and think about the feelings they might create for your audience. If you don't feel like drawing, use your fingers to make a camera frame like the one on page 6, and move it closer and further from your eye to see the three different frames in real life.

STORYBOARDS

Now that you know how you're going to set up your shot, let's **shoot some takes**, which is the word people use to identify each time they film a scene. You can't just shout "START!" because there are way too many people wearing way too many hats for everybody to start at the same time.

TRICK #16:   LEARN THE CODE.

So instead, you or one of your team shouts out these phrases in this order:
"Quiet on set!"
"Roll sound!"
"Roll camera!"
"Marker!"
"Action!"

This code lets everybody know that you are capturing a **take** for your movie. Here's what these phrases mean:

★ **"Quiet on set!"** This is for everyone so they stop talking, moving around, or eating noisy snacks.

★ **"Roll sound!"** This is to tell your sound person to start recording. They might answer you with the word "Speeding!"

★ **"Roll camera!"** This is to tell your camera person to start filming. They might respond to you by saying "Rolling!"

★ **"Marker!"** This is for one of your P.A.s or assistant camera people, to remind them to hold that slate board in front of the camera.

★ Now stop for a brief dramatic pause—this alerts your actors who are waiting to perform.

★ **"Action!"** And then the magic happens! You and your crew stand quietly behind the camera and lights while your actors pretend as hard as they can.

But then—when is the take over? When do you call out "Cut!" as loudly as you can to stop and then do it again? That's another one of those decisions a director makes. Feeling like that's a lot of pressure? You're right. But here's a trick that might help:

TRICK #17: LET IT ROLL.

Not that long ago, movies were shot on **film**, so they were made of real pictures. Every second of a film-shot movie was made up of 24 different pictures, or images, and an hour-long movie was made up of 86,400 images, one after the other. Real film is expensive. Filmmakers would do everything they could not to waste film by shooting bad takes.

But now the only thing you need to worry about is how much space you have on the hard drive of your camera or phone. You don't have to end a take where you told your actors you would; instead, you can watch them finish their lines and live in the moment. See if they **improvise**, which is a great word that means to make something up that wasn't in the script. You never know what might happen when you let it roll.

PUT ON YOUR GAFFER HAT

Go watch a scene from one of your favorite movies that takes place at night. How is the action lit? Are they using **practical lights**—lights that would normally be there, like street lamps and car headlights or **clips** of a full moon?

What is the lighting in this movie teaching you about the story?

Is it starting to sound like making a movie is all about managing other people? Would you be more interested in an animated approach to making films?

TRICK #18: ANIMATION: BUILD YOUR PERFECT WORLD.

Once upon a time, before about 30 years ago, **animation** took forever! Artists would turn gray toiling at a drafting table, painstakingly drawing cartoon characters making their every move—sitting, standing, running, chasing each other, falling off cliffs, and so on, and so on. But now programs like **Pencil2D** (pencil2d.github.io), **CreaToon** (creatoon.en.softonic.com), and **Stykz** (stykz.net) make creating an animated film much easier. And if you're interested in animating a movie, then making storyboards is going to be an even more important skill for you to practice. Unlike a live-action movie, with real actors on set, you won't be able to let it roll (Trick #17, page 51). Instead you'll design, draw, and animate your reality. (We've included extra storyboard pages in the back to help you get started.)

You'll be free to create a world as wild as your zaniest idea. Such freedom can be great, but may also lead to too many options, which can be scary! But don't worry. Here is a trick to help you focus your imagination:

TRICK #19: MAKE SOME RULES.

If you make some simple rules for yourself, your story, animation, and even your creative process, is going to get easier. For instance, try limiting the colors you use to just three. Here's an example with red, brown, and yellow.

There's a little reddish person in front of a little yellow house.

There's a little brown car parked in the driveway.

And it looks like a little yellow package has arrived.

What a boring world we've created, which means it's a perfect time to:

TRICK #20: **BREAK SOME RULES.**

With a unicorn!!!

Not all rules are meant to be broken, but it can be incredibly satisfying to break the creative ones. This is what happens in musicals when someone starts to sing. The rule is, "We are normal people and normal people just talk." But suddenly a big feeling comes along and breaks the rules, and a character must look right at the audience, or the camera, and SING.

One last production trick: Have a snack. Why?

TRICK #21:   SNACKS PROVIDE ANSWERS.

Whether you're surrounded by the contained chaos of a movie set or sitting with the contained chaos of your own brain while animating, avoid hunger! On some movie sets, there are tables and tables and tables of snacks! Sweet, salty, hot, spicy, cold, and, yes, even healthy snacks! This is called **craft service** or **crafty**. Snacks are provided so the cast and crew don't go hungry and make hungry decisions. Hungry decisions are quick, impulsive decisions you may regret later. Also: The right snack can give you time to think up an answer to a question you're not sure about!

Here is a suggested layout for your film set craft table:

- ★ Keep carrots away from Cheetos to avoid confusion.
- ★ Provide a spoon for loose or unwrapped items to prevent the spread of germs.
- ★ Keep cold stuff away from hot stuff.
- ★ Make sure water is an option.
- ★ Sodas tend to only make you want to drink more soda; best to hide them under the table.
- ★ Have lots of small cups for your crew to take snacks back to the set with them.
- ★ Sweet goes well with salty. Creamy goes well with spicy. And everybody loves cake!

Now that you've shot your movie and eaten several tables' worth of treats, what comes next? It's time to finish your monster, flip the switch, and bring it to life with post-production.

POST-PRODUCTION CHAPTER

EDITING AND SCORING
THE IDEA

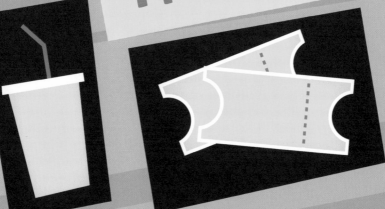

Let's organize the footage, create a **score** (the accompanying music), and otherwise finish your movie! You already have a bunch of uncut takes on your computer or phone. Now it's time to **edit**: take the best parts and put them together to tell your story. Or, if you want a **metaphor** for it, it's a little like taking a garden of vegetables and turning them into one salad. Chances are you're going to leave a lot out of the final bowl!

Editing is an amazing process. Programs like Final Cut, Adobe Premiere Pro, and iMovie make it much easier to edit yourself. Wearing an Editor Hat gives you the ultimate control over the final product, but also requires a lot of focus and attention to detail. This is one of the reasons that directors work with an editor. Especially an editor who wasn't on set and only sees the takes you captured. If you are working with an editor, I have a trick for you:

TRICK #22: BE TOO NICE.

Being a film editor is often a thankless job. A director may just show up and tell you (impolitely) what edits they need. So, future directors, don't do that. Be nice. Be *too* nice. Because knowing a great editor will make all your future projects better. If you're the editor this time around, be nice to yourself. Here are a few other tricks for you:

TRICK #23: MAKE THE MOVIE YOU ARE ALREADY MAKING.

You will probably always feel like you could have made your movie better. Especially when you're editing, the little things that bothered you during production are hard to ignore. You might want to reshoot a chase scene, you might want to recast the whole thing with different actors, you might want to rewrite the part of the script that never felt perfect. But even if you can start over, DON'T! Keep making the best version of the movie you're already making. It might take a weekend or a year, but when you're done, the whole process will end up as a great behind-the-scenes story in itself—about the story you wanted to tell.

This is NOT a trick that makes it seem like less is expected from you than would be expected of an adult. On the contrary: You as a kid have more imagination before breakfast than most adults have in a month. But this goes both ways. Don't give up on a movie because you can imagine doing some of it better. What I am saying is: Finish your movie and use what you learned in finishing it on your NEXT movie.

A good trick for finishing a movie is:

TRICK #24:   DEADLINES ARE A LIFESAVER.

There is no right amount of time to edit, score, and finish a movie. There is only what you think is the right time. Too much time and you might lose interest. Too little and you will feel rushed. I suggest making weekly deadlines. You decide what you still need to do on your movie and get at least one thing done every week.

There's a calendar you can use on the next two pages. The months are blank so you can start working now and not wait until January of the next year. Three months might feel like a long time, but trust me, it will go a lot faster without some deadlines!

Suggestions:

★ Budget some goofing-around time *away* from your project to gain fresh perspective.

★ Try planning *two* deadlines for one of the weeks.

★ Do you have a family get-together coming up where you can share your latest draft? Add that to your schedule.

MONTH 1

To-do	Deadline	To-do	Deadline
	☐		☐
	☐		☐
	☐		☐
	☐		☐

MONTH 2

To-do	Deadline	To-do	Deadline
	☐		☐
	☐		☐
	☐		☐
	☐		☐

MONTH 3

To-do	Deadline	To-do	Deadline
	☐		☐
	☐		☐
	☐		☐
	☐		☐

MONTH 1

To-do	Deadline	To-do	Deadline
	☐		☐
	☐		☐
	☐		☐
	☐		☐

MONTH 2

To-do	Deadline	To-do	Deadline
	☐		☐
	☐		☐
	☐		☐
	☐		☐

MONTH 3

To-do	Deadline	To-do	Deadline
	☐		☐
	☐		☐
	☐		☐
	☐		☐

Now let's look at the nuts and bolts of your edit. There are a few tricks you can use. Let's say you have this great scene between two characters, Todd (remember him?) and a cashier at the supermarket.

INT. CONVENIENCE STORE - NIGHT

Todd, his mouth watering, walks up to the counter with a carton of premium strawberry ice cream. Yum! The cashier rings it up.

                    CASHIER
          That will be three dollars.

Todd reaches into his pocket. Looks up, panicked.

                    TODD
     I, uh, don't have any money!

                    CASHIER
     Then, uh, you don't get any ice cream.

                    TODD
     PLEEEAASE! I NEED this ice cream!

The cashier looks at Todd.

                    CASHIER
          Pleeeaase. Leave.

Devastated, Todd lowers his head and walks out of the store.

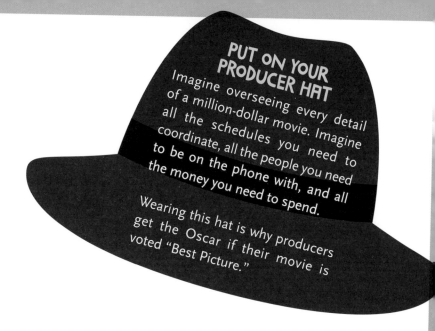

Let's say you have two takes of this scene that you like. In the first one, the actor playing Todd is amazing, he acts his face off . . . except after the "PLEEEAASE!" he sort of *smiles*! Oh NO! A smile? The character Todd would NOT smile, he's desperate for strawberry ice cream!

In the second take, your actor is only *sort of okay*. (Maybe he was distracted; maybe he was hungry for a craft table snack. Refer to Trick #21, page 54.) Regardless of the reason, the take is just not as good. But at least, after the "PLEEEAASE!" he did not smile.

What do you do?

TRICK #25:   CUT TO A REACTION.

Midway through Todd screaming, "PLEEEAASE!" cut to the cashier. Show the cashier's reaction to Todd's yelling before you cut back to Todd. That way you can use the best parts of each performance, which might occur in several different takes.

Here is another way to help you decide where to cut your **footage**:

TRICK #26: FOLLOW THE ACTION.

Our eyes will always be drawn to things in motion. This trait may be left over from ancient times, when early humans always had to be on guard, scanning their surroundings to avoid wildebeest stampedes. You, sitting safely at your computer, need to make use of this fact. So—keep movement in your movie. But keep it clear and organized around your story. If there's a big romantic moment, but a Canadian goose flies by, honking in the background, your audience is going to have a hard time not watching *that*. And speaking of watching, the last editing trick is:

TRICK #27: GET FRESH EYES.

Wait! Before you start Googling "eye transplants," let me explain. Go find a friend, enemy, or frenemy and ask them to view your project. The key to this: Don't tell them anything before you press "Play." You can always explain something that's missing later, but first, try and get their unbiased feedback, their "fresh eyes" and honest viewpoint. Such comments are also called **notes**. But when they tell you what they think, remember: You asked for it.

There is nothing worse than being asked for honesty, giving it, and then realizing that what the person who asked you *really* wanted was compliments. Just in case this happens to you, here is a list of compliments you can give pretty much any filmmaker:

- ★ "Such believable characters!"
- ★ "Such a dynamic story!"
- ★ "Wow. Really fresh!"
- ★ "What a great twist!"
- ★ "Love that pineapple car!"

PUT ON YOUR EDITOR HAT

Go watch an action scene from a blockbuster movie. Turn the sound off and count the number of cuts. Does each cut switch between different takes? Do the cuts show a character's reaction to the action? Do the cuts make you feel like everything is moving faster than it really is? Or, are there no cuts?

Movie: _____

Scene: _____

Number of cuts: _____

Now that your movie is put together, let's talk about the **score**: the music that accompanies each scene. Music is incredibly powerful. Music can affect the tone and emotion of a scene. Music can affect the pace and energy of a scene. Basically, music can affect everything in a scene. It is a great tool to use in movies. In fact, movie scores are often the first thing people think about. Like:

★ *Star Wars*. Are you thinking about it? I am.
★ *The Lion King*. I know what I'm thinking about and it rhymes with "Urkle of Knife."
★ *Jaws*. Even if you haven't seen it, I bet you can do an impression of the "duh duh!"

PUT ON YOUR COMPOSER HAT

Watch a scene right at the end of an emotional movie. Hopefully someone is crying. Try to just listen to the music. Then watch the scene again and just listen to the **dialogue** (what's being said).

What is the music trying to make you feel? Now go back 20 or 30 minutes into the movie, and do the same exercise with the characters when they are having a great time. What would happen if you switched the music between those two scenes?

Of course, your movie should get a score as well. So, if you go to LETSMAKEAMOVIERIGHTNOW.com you can find five different movie scores you can use right now for free. Put them in your short films or movies and if anyone asks you about them, send them to the website. Just cut them up, loop them, or use the whole thing.

If you're going to write your own score, I have a trick for you.

TRICK #28:   **HEARTBEAT ... HEARTBEAT ... HEART**

This trick has two meanings. **The first meaning is about is about how patterns work in music.** If a song or musical phrase feels "finished," humans tend to feel satisfied. It's called **the resolve**. But if that same piece of music feels "unfinished," humans tend to feel stressed, worried, unsure, or anxious. Use this trick when writing your music to help the audience feel the way you want them to.

The second meaning of this trick is about the word "heartbeat." If you're making a movie with a scary or intense moment, try using the sound of a heartbeat in your score. This will make your audience feel as if they can hear the pounding of their own hearts!

Bottom line, you need to make or use music to help tell your story.

Movie sounds

You don't have to stop making sounds once you've scored your movie. You can go back into the edited version and add **Foley sounds**. Foley sounds are sounds made to emulate things like squeaky shoes, hand slaps, key turns, door knocks, punches, sizzles, shots, hoofbeats, and blastoffs—sounds that don't get recorded on set during filming.

Now that you have edited your movie, gotten notes from a friend, re-edited your movie, gotten notes from an enemy, re-edited your movie, and scored your movie, what comes next?

It's time to show the world! We call that part **distribution**.

DISTRIBUTION CHAPTER

SHARING THE IDEA

Let's get this movie seen! There are a couple of ways to share your work. You can do it one-on-one in your living room with a special event: the **premiere** screening of the one-and-only copy of your masterpiece. OR you can use the most powerful instrument of sharing the world has ever known—the Internet!

The Internet can be great, but it can also be mean. Check with an adult before you share your movie online.

Streaming

When you and an adult set up an account (as on YouTube) to share your films, you might want to name your page something like, "YOUR NAME Productions." Using the word "Productions" will you help you set an expectation that your audience is about to see something important.

Remember to keep adding material on a weekly or monthly basis. This is the fastest way to cultivate an active fan base. Don't freak out! Weekly videos don't have to be finished films; they could be a short video of you talking about making your movie.

Everybody loves behind-the-scenes content because it makes them feel like they're part of the process.

No matter what you post, I have a trick for you:

TRICK #29:   CHECK THE VIEWS, NOT THE COMMENTS.

The nicest comment may only last as long as it takes you to read it, while the meanest comment may linger in your mind. Let me remind you that you are the writer and director and editor (and maybe D.P., sound, actor, costumes, makeup, and crafty) for your movie! You spent your time creating something amazing that will last. When you scroll through a nasty comment from someone you know or someone you've never met, remember: They didn't direct, or film, or properly light, or edit, or score, or write. They've got nothing on you! Some sites let you turn off comments, which you might want to do.

Views, on the other hand, are awesome! They only count the number of computers, phones, tablets, and devices of people who watched your movie. It's a fun number to watch grow. Here's a trick to help you grow it:

TRICK #30:   #WORDSARESEARCHABLE

When you upload your movie, you are not done! For however long as you spent making it, spend at least 20 minutes filling in the "About" section of your movie. The more words in that section, the higher the chances that it will pop up for future fans.

Here's a possible list of things to include in that section:

★ The script for fans to read.

★ The cast list.

★ The crew list.

★ Some of your influences.

★ A short review of this book and how it helped you make a movie. #letsmakeamoviethebook

★ And "Thank yous" to everyone who helped . . . which brings us to the last trick:

DON'T WAIT FOR THE ACADEMY AWARDS TO THANK YOUR FRIENDS AND FAMILY.

They believed in you from the start. Maybe they bought you this book. Maybe they let you use their phone or computer. Maybe they fed you and your crew. Maybe all they did was get out of your way and let you create. No matter how they helped, find a way to thank them. In the movie business, one way you can say thanks is by giving **Producer credits**. It's your way of letting the world know who helped you. You can also give **Executive Producer credits** for parents, guardians, and others who were *extra* helpful to the movie! Maybe they'd be even more likely to let you decorate the garage to look like an alien cave for your next movie.

PUT ON YOUR EXECUTIVE PRODUCER HAT

Make a list of the people you know and what filmmaking hat YOU think they would wear well. Now for extra points—go convince them to be part of your next movie!

This is like the Boss level of filmmaking, when you help put teams of creative people together to make movies happen.

Now that you've written a movie, directed a movie, edited a movie, and released a movie, what comes next? You start back at the beginning of this book with your next great idea!

Or maybe you and your crew are up for a different creative endeavor . . .

HERE'S A BLANK PAGE...

THE LONG WEEKEND SHORT FiLM CHALLENGE

You have a long weekend coming—a holiday weekend, vacation weekend, summer weekend, etc.—and a whole lot of ideas!

READY. SET.
LET'S MAKE A MOViE!

Here are five different movie prompts, and tons of space for your script ideas, storyboards, and movie notes.

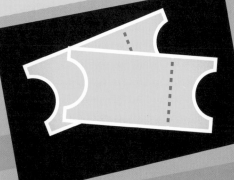

AN IMPOSSIBLE CHALLENGE MEETS AN UNSTOPPABLE FOOL.

MAKE A COMEDY

During your next long weekend: Can you make a film about a likable weirdo and his or her attempt to do something amazing?

You will need:

★ 1–3 characters

★ 2–3 locations

★ 1 impossible task

★ 1 wild ride

My story is about: A _____ character

being changed by a _____ in a

_____.

My character wants _____ more than

anything in the world.

My character will get help from _____ and

_____.

My character's catchphrase that they always say when things get tough is,

" _____ ,"

The big lesson my character is going to learn about themselves is

_____.

COMEDY TRICK: "YES, AND . . ."

In comedy, and especially in improvised comedy, the rule is, you always say "Yes, and . . ." That means you agree with the idea of the other person and then you add to it.

"We are in a boat!"

"Yes, and it is sinking!"

"Yes, and those are sharks!"

"Yes, and I'm the King of the Sharks, so we're saved!"

"Yes, and . . ." helps you take a silly scenario and make it even crazier. The only time you should break this rule is when a character "plays it straight." They might say something like, "This is a bad idea," or "How's this gonna work?" Basically, that character is saying what your audience might already be thinking.

Three-Act Comedy Structure
Act 1: Beginning

★ Introduce the character and what makes them likable.

★ (Maybe meet their friend, or friends.)

★ Discover the main character's big problem! In a comedy, the big problem is wrapped up in your character's personality quirks.

Act 2: Middle

★ The character tries to solve the problem and fails!

★ The character tries to solve the problem and fails!

★ The character tries something new and weird to solve their problem and . . .

Act 3: End

★ THEY DON'T FAIL!

★ There is celebrating, exciting music, and sometimes even kissing.

COMEDY NOTES

COMEDY STORYBOARDS

SCENE:

NOTES:

SCENE:

NOTES:

SCENE:

NOTES:

SCENE:

NOTES:

SCENE:

NOTES:

SCENE:

NOTES:

SCENE:

NOTES:

SCENE:

NOTES:

SCENE:

NOTES:

SCENE:

NOTES:

SCENE:

NOTES:

SCENE:

NOTES:

WHAT'S OUT THERE?
MAKE A GHOST STORY

During your next long weekend: Can you tell a story of a likable group of friends who are haunted by a terrifying force?

You will need:

★ 3–4 characters

★ 1 spooky location

★ 5 special effects

★ 1 big reveal

My story is about: A group of _____

characters being changed by a _____

in a _____,

My characters want _____ more than

anything in the world.

My characters will have to split up when they find _____

_____.

My characters are haunted by _____.

The haunting creature, ghost, or monster was created when

_____ and will not stop until it gets

_____.

GHOST STORY TRICK: TINY TERRORS AND ONE BIG REVEAL

One of the best things about a horror film is its creature or creatures. Seeing the terrifying monster, the slathering werewolf, or the freaky clown is what gets people in theater seats. But the scariest, most exciting part is the build-up to the reveal. This is when you give your audience glimpses of your ghost or monster, but not the beast itself. Scaring the audience in this way is sometimes called fear conditioning, and (sort of like our attraction to things in motion; see Trick #26, page 62), it's based on long-evolved abilities to discern and react to things that might cause us harm. Startle your audience with small things: a door slamming on its own, a glass sliding off a table and shattering, a loud clock stopping—and build up to that panicked chase through the graveyard.

Three-Act Ghost Story Structure

Act 1: Beginning

* ★ Introduce the characters. Make them different from each other.
* ★ Take them to a new location.
* ★ Create a reason they are forced to stay there. This can be as simple as "All the doors are locked!" or as complicated as, "We have a responsibility to take care of this location."

Act 2: Middle

* ★ The characters notice something strange.
* ★ The characters feel something strange.
* ★ The characters begin to act strange.

Act 3: End

* ★ Aaah! Reveal the ghost!
* ★ Do they escape? (You can answer this question, or leave it hanging and let your audience decide.)

GHOST STORY NOTES

GHOST STORY STORYBOARDS

SCENE:

NOTES:

SCENE:

NOTES:

SCENE:

NOTES:

SCENE:

NOTES:

SCENE:

NOTES:

SCENE:

NOTES:

SCENE:

NOTES:

SCENE:

NOTES:

SCENE:

NOTES:

SCENE:

NOTES:

SCENE:

NOTES:

SCENE:

NOTES:

BUT WHAT REALLY HAPPENED?
MAKE A DOCUMENTARY

During your next long weekend: Can you tell the story of a true or imaginary event using interviews and reenactments?

You will need:
- ★ 1 event
- ★ 2–20 opinions about it

My story is about: The _____ event.

People who feel one way about it _____,

People who feel a different way about it _____

_____,

How do you feel about it? _____

_____

(Will that be in the Documentary?)

DOCUMENTARY TRICK: **LEAVE "SPACE" BEFORE AND AFTER YOUR QUESTIONS AND THEIR ANSWERS.**

Making a documentary about a real event or a "**mockumentary**" about a fake event can be great ways to get started in moviemaking. Instead of running around chasing actors, the people you interview will act like themselves, which is sometimes easier. Interview a variety of people about your subject, then edit their answers together to create a story. Make sure you leave lots of **airtime** before and after your questions and their answers. There is nothing worse when editing a documentary than not being able to use someone's perfect answer because you are still talking underneath it.

Three-Act Documentary Structure

Act 1: Beginning

> ★ Introduce the topic.

Act 2: Middle

> ★ Let the people you interview address the topic from lots of different perspectives.

Act 3: End

> ★ Make a decision about the topic or leave your opinion out of it.

DOCUMENTARY NOTES

DOCUMENTARY NOTES

DOCUMENTARY STORYBOARDS

SCENE:

NOTES:

SCENE:

NOTES:

SCENE:

NOTES:

SCENE:

NOTES:

SCENE:

NOTES:

SCENE:

NOTES:

SCENE:

NOTES:

SCENE:

NOTES:

SCENE:

NOTES:

SCENE:

NOTES:

SCENE:

NOTES:

SCENE:

NOTES:

NUMBER 4

Go, Go, Go, Go, Go!
MAKE AN ACTION MOViE

During your next long weekend: Can you tell a thrilling story about a character who gets everything exactly right at exactly the right moment?

You will need:
- ★ 1 main character
- ★ 2–3 people who stand in his or her way
- ★ 1 chase scene
- ★ 1 piece of valuable information

My story is about: A _____ character

changed with a _____ in a _____

_____.

My character wants _____ more than

anything in the world.

My character is running from _____,

My character has a special skill for _____,

This skill is going to come in handy when _____

and when _____ and when

_____.

If my character fails, this terrible thing will happen: _____

_____.

ACTiON TRICK: SPEED COMES FROM EDITING.

The crazier you want this film to be, the more in control you need to be. If your character is going to run, and punch, and dive, and climb, film your movie in pieces and then use the magic of editing to make it feel fast and out of control. If you end up with pauses within the action, you can always throw in a reaction shot: maybe one of your hero looking over his shoulder or scanning city rooftops for bad guys.

Music will also help. Try picking a fast-paced song you like and edit to it. The beat will stay the same and you can follow the rhythm. If you pick the song before you film, you can even have your actor run along to the beat. Decide later whether you want to (or can) keep the song or replace it with your own score.

Three-Act Action Movie Structure
Act 1: Beginning

★ Introduce the main character and **set up** what they must accomplish.

★ Their task should be as difficult as possible within a limited time frame and countless obstacles. You can also make the task appear very simple and then reveal many complications, one at a time. This kind of slow reveal might make your character turn to the camera and say, "You gotta be kidding me!"

Act 2: Middle

★ The character nearly fails!

★ The character nearly fails again!

★ The character comes face-to-face with the toughest challenge yet and . . .

Act 3: End

★ Nearly FAILS!

★ Then, after one more little challenge they somehow knew was coming, they SUCCEED!

ACTION MOVIE NOTES

ACTiON MOViE STORYBOARDS

SCENE:

NOTES: ....

SCENE:

NOTES: ....

SCENE:

NOTES:

SCENE:

NOTES:

SCENE:

NOTES:

SCENE:

NOTES:

SCENE:

NOTES:

SCENE:

NOTES:

SCENE:

NOTES:

....
....
....

SCENE:

NOTES:

....
....

SCENE:

NOTES:

SCENE:

NOTES:

THE WORLD iS NOT GOiNG TO SAVE iTSELF.
MAKE A SUPERHERO MOViE

During your next long weekend: Can you tell an exciting story about an unlikely hero discovering their secret magic?

You will need:
- ★ 1 main character
- ★ 1 super-charged object, home world, or set of parents
- ★ 1 chance to prove themselves
- ★ 1 plan for the future

My story is about: A _____ character

changed by a _____ in a

_____.

My character always thought they wanted _____

more than anything in the world.

My character discovers they have _____

power and it comes from _____.

My character is tested in a small way with/by _____

_____ and they nearly fail.

My character will practice with/by _____

until they get better at their power.

My character is going to be TESTED in a BIG WAY soon, and they feel

_____ about it.

SUPERHERO MOVIE TRICK: GOTTA HAVE A MONTAGE!

The fastest way to go from Zero to Hero is with a music video. In filmmaking, we call this a **montage**. Montage is a French word that means editing together lots of little scenes to make one big one. It's like a micro-movie mid-film that shows a character learning and growing. Show your hero trying to use his or her power and failing. Then you add practice, ability, and confidence. Works every time! Music is super important to the montage. Find something upbeat and hopeful with lots of high singing.

Three-Act Superhero Movie Structure
Act 1: Beginning

★ Introduce the main character and show how boring they are.

★ Introduce a small discovery about where they're from or who their parents are.

★ Include a highly emotional moment that causes them to demonstrate a secret magic.

Act 2: Middle

★ The main character tests the new-found magic.

★ They practice this magic.

★ They decide not to use this magic; it's become too powerful. This critical moment in a story is sometimes called the **dark midnight of the soul**. It is when your character lives in their fears and doubts. Having this difficult moment in your story will help your character earn their future successes.

Act 3: End

★ An event in the main character's life forces them to use their powers.

★ A hero is born!

SUPERHERO MOVIE NOTES

SUPERHERO MOVIE STORYBOARDS

SCENE:

NOTES:

SCENE:

NOTES:

SCENE:

NOTES:

SCENE:

NOTES:

SCENE:

NOTES:

SCENE:

NOTES:

SCENE:

NOTES:

SCENE:

NOTES:

SCENE:

NOTES:

SCENE:

NOTES:

SCENE:

NOTES:

SCENE:

NOTES:

STORYBOARD PAGES

SKETCHING THE IDEA

SCENE:

NOTES:

SCENE:

NOTES:

SCENE:

NOTES:

SCENE:

NOTES:

SCENE:

NOTES:

SCENE:

NOTES:

SCENE:

NOTES:

SCENE:

NOTES:

SCENE:

NOTES:

SCENE:

NOTES:

SCENE:

NOTES:

....
....
....

SCENE:

NOTES:

....
....

SCENE:

NOTES:

SCENE:

NOTES:

SCENE:

NOTES:

SCENE:

NOTES:

SCENE:

NOTES:

SCENE:

NOTES:

SCENE:

NOTES:

SCENE:

NOTES:

SCENE:

NOTES: ....

....

....

SCENE:

NOTES: ....

....

SCENE:

NOTES:

SCENE:

NOTES:

SCENE:

NOTES:

SCENE:

NOTES:

SCENE:

NOTES:

SCENE:

NOTES:

SCENE:

NOTES:

SCENE:

NOTES:

SCENE:

NOTES:

SCENE:

NOTES:

SCENE:

NOTES:

SCENE:

NOTES:

SCENE:

NOTES:

SCENE:

NOTES:

SCENE:

NOTES:

SCENE:

NOTES:

SCENE:

NOTES:

SCENE:

NOTES:

SCENE:

NOTES:
....
....
....

SCENE:

NOTES:
....
....
....

SCENE:

NOTES:

SCENE:

NOTES:

SCENE:

NOTES:

SCENE:

NOTES:

SCENE:

NOTES:

SCENE:

NOTES:

SCENE:

NOTES:

SCENE:

NOTES:

SCENE:

NOTES:
....
....
....

SCENE:

NOTES:
....
....

SCENE:

NOTES: ....

....

....

SCENE:

NOTES: ....

....

....

SCENE:

NOTES:

SCENE:

NOTES:

SCENE:

NOTES:

SCENE:

NOTES:

GLOSSARY OF MOVIEMAKING TERMS

Act. A section of a movie or play that has its own small story, yet also furthers the main story.

Actors. The nicest, meanest, loudest, quietest, craziest, or most normal people in the room, depending on what you ask them to do.

Airtime. The time a program or production is scheduled to air.

Animation. The long-term slow-motion process of creating a film, one picture at a time, with drawings. Or the slightly faster slow-motion process of creating a film with computers.

Anti-hero. The "complicated" character that an audience hopes succeeds and fails at the same time.

Apple box. A sturdy wooden box an actor stands on to make a shot better or just to look taller. **Half apple.** A sturdy wooden box that is half as tall as an apple box. Used for the same reason as an apple box. **Pancake.** A sturdy wooden box that measures an inch high. Also used for the same reason as an apple box.

Audition. A place where actors show you their talents by performing parts of songs or scenes.

Back to one. When you reset your filming back to the beginning and start again.

Blocking a shot. When the movie's director and director of photography walk through what's about to happen, and tell the actors how they'll need to film for a shot.

Cast. The group of actors who perform in a movie.

Casting Director. Works with the director and producer to find the perfect actors for each role in a movie.

Clips. Short pieces of video footage.

Close up. A camera frame that focuses on the subject not the background. Good for showing details.

Collaborators. People you trust to multiply their ideas with yours for incredible results.

Costumer. The person responsible for dressing actors in the appropriate outfits and making sure their outfits look the same throughout the whole time they are filming.

Craft service. Those responsible for providing food service for the cast and crew during filming. Also called "Crafty."

Crew. The team that works on the technical elements of a movie, such as the lights, camera, sound, makeup, and costumes.

Dark Midnight of the Soul. The portion of a story when all seems lost for your hero.

Deadlines. The date or time you must be finished with something. Deadlines are often set by a teacher, a boss, or a personal schedule.

Dialogue. The conversation that takes place in a film.

Director. The person at the helm, or the person who is steering the movie. He or she is responsible for the ultimate creative vision of the film project.

Director of Photography (D.P.). The person responsible for filming the best possible version of the director's vision of a film.

Distribution. The process of getting a movie seen by selling it, sharing it, or having it stolen by Internet pirates.

Documentary. A video or film presentation about a factual event or topic.

Editing. Selecting shots and putting them together to create a finished film.

Evolution. A process of incremental transformation in living things and their behaviors.

Exceeding expectations. The act of impressing people by doing more than they thought you could.

Executive Producer. The person in charge of producing the movie, by providing the team needed to make the film. Not involved in technical aspects, but oversees overall production. Usually involved on the business/finance end of filmmaking.

Fear conditioning. When we learn to recognize and even predict events or entities that might do us harm.

Film. A feature film of about 80 minutes or more. OR: Thin, flexible lengths of material covered in chemicals that enable images to be captured photographically.

Foley sounds. Sounds made up and added to a movie after it is shot to make it feel more real.

Footage. Sections of unedited film or video material.

Frame. One of the many still images which compose the complete movie.

Franchise. In movies, a series of films featuring a specific character or characters.

Gaffer. The person responsible for lighting a film set as the D.P. wants it to be.

Hero. The "good" character that an audience is meant to root for. Also known as the Protagonist.

Improvise. Making up a creative work, such as a speech, a poem, or a comedy routine, on the spur of the moment.

Internet. A sprawling ocean of ideas, a constantly self-updating review of humanity's existence in the known universe and its desire to understand and reimagine itself.

Landscape. The lengthwise or horizontal framing of a shot on a phone, tablet, or camera.

Makeup Artist. The person responsible for how an actor looks for a film shoot. They might create makeup and hairstyling to make an actor beautiful, or makeup to make an actor frightening and monster-like.

Metaphor. A way of comparing two things, saying that one thing "IS" the other thing. Example: My friend IS a rock. (Meaning your friend can be dependable, thick-headed, and immovable.)

Mockumentary. Fictional facts, events, or subjects presented in the form of a documentary.

Montage. A series of shots showing something happening over a period, such as a person becoming stronger, people exploring and enjoying a new place, and so on.

Movie. A story or event recorded by a camera (on a phone or otherwise).

Music. A thoughtful combination of rhythm, tone, and feeling.

Notes. Comments and criticisms given to a screenwriter or filmmaker that suggest ideas that will improve a project.

Picture. An old-timey word meaning "a movie."

Post production. The part of the filmmaking process that happens after you've finished filming your initial material. This includes such things as **editing** and creating a **score**.

Practical lights. Illumination that already exists within your film frame: lamp lights, streetlights, moonlight, etc.

Premiere. The very first time a movie is shown, either to a specially selected audience or to the public.

Producer. The person responsible for all the logistics of a film project, as well as the budget and schedule.

Production. The time spent filming, also called **the shoot**.

Production Assistant (P.A.). The person responsible for many diverse tasks on set. This position is the "Swiss army knife" of crew jobs.

Protagonist. Hero or heroine—your leading character.

Pull out. When the camera backs away from the subject, making it appear smaller.

Push in. When the camera closes in on the subject, making its features appear larger.

Rack focus. When the camera shifts focus from one subject to another.

Resolve, the. The natural completion of a musical phrase by its return to its first note in the appropriate scale.

Reveal. When you finally reveal what a subject, such as a monster, truly looks like.

Scene. A unit of film action; action that takes place continually in one location.

Score. The music that goes with the movie visuals to add dramatic feeling.

Screenplay. The script of your movie filled in with descriptions of setting/location, time of day, characters, action, and **dialogue**.

Script. A story told in the order it is meant to be seen; a **screenplay**.

Set up. The introduction of your character, his or her world, and the problem they must solve.

Shoot, the. The day or days of filming, also called **production**.

Shoot some takes. Filming a few versions of the same **scene**.

Shot. A sequence of a movie filmed from beginning to end with one camera.

Side. A brief section of a script acted out by an actor in an audition.

Slate board. Also, known as a **slate**, **clapperboard**, **sound marker**, and other names. The P.A. uses this board. She or he writes down what scene you are filming and the take number. The board is clapped or snapped with each take and filmed. The editor can use the filmed board and its sound later to sync the film.

Sound Editor. The person responsible for recording the sound on the film set with a boom microphone or "mic" (sounds like "Mike") or many individual microphones.

Squared off: A phrase meaning the camera is locked in place and pointed directly at the action.

Storyboard. Comics that show what will happen in each shot and how a camera can capture the best version of it.

Take. One filmed version of a scene.

That's a wrap. A phrase that means the filming is over.

That's a wrap on (name of actor). This means a particular actor is done filming.

Three-act structure. How most stories and movies are told: Act 1 is the beginning, Act 2 is the middle, and Act 3 is the end.

Tragedy. A sad story where a character doesn't get what they want in the end. OR: A sad story where a character gets what they wanted, but learns it was not actually what they wanted at all.

Villain. The "bad" character you want your audience to root against.

Whip pan. When the camera moves quickly away from the subject (used at the end of scenes).

Wide shot. A camera frame that is taken from far away, and should include lots of background. Good for establishing where you are.

Wrap party. A party you throw once you've finished filming your movie. It's a great way to thank your awesome crew.

Writer's block. When you're trying so hard to come up with a good idea that you don't come up with any.

HELPFUL MOViEMAKING RESOURCES

Adobe Premiere Pro. adobe.com/products/premiere
Professional video editing software. The company charges a monthly fee.

CreaToon. creatoon.en.softonic.com
Easy-to-use free animation software that lets you create 2D cut-out-style animations frame by frame.

DubScript. dubscript.com
This is a screenplay editor for Android phones and tablets.

Final Draft. finaldraft.com
Professional screenwriting software. The company offers an educational discount.

iMovie. apple.com/imovie
Apple movie editing software available for free with the purchase of a Mac computer.

No Film School. nofilmschool.com
A community of independent filmmakers and creatives learning from each other.

Plotbot. plotbot.com
A free script writing website. Write from any browser by yourself or with collaborators. You can keep your work private with invited friends, or make your work public and meet new collaborators.

Stykz. stykz.net
Free animation software that lets you make cartoons with stick figures.

Toontastic. toontastic.withgoogle.com
Turn your ideas into 3D cartoons. This animation app lets you tell stories with customizable characters. Plot your story, animate it, and add a soundtrack.

WriterDuet. writerduet.com
A scriptwriting website that allows you to write online from anywhere, use professional formatting, save up to three scripts, and write with collaborators. It offers a free version, as well as more advanced paid version. If you need the full program, tell them you have this book and they will offer you a student discount code.

ALL YOUR NEW TRICKS IN ONE PLACE

Trick #1: Go your own way!

Trick #2: Save your ideas!

Trick #3: "Good writers borrow but great writers steal."

Trick #4: There are no new stories, just new tellings.

Trick #5: Act 1—Make your hero someone we root for.

Trick #6: Act 2—One lock and three bad keys

Trick #7: Act 3— Too much of a good thing

Trick #8: See the movie before you make the movie.

Trick #9: Start with what is true for you!

Trick #10: Write it right.

Trick #11: Every idea is your best idea...until the next idea!

Trick #12: Know what hat you're wearing.

Trick #13: Movies are a great team sport.

Trick #14: Turn that phone!

Trick #15: Set the shot.

Trick #16: Learn the code.

Trick #17: Let it roll.

Trick #18: Animation: build your perfect world.

Trick #19: Make some rules.

Trick #20: Break some rules.

Trick #21: Snacks provide answers.

Trick #22: Be too nice.

Trick #23: Make the movie you are already making.

Trick #24: Deadlines are a lifesaver.

Trick #25: Cut to a reaction.

Trick #26: Follow the action.

Trick #27: Get fresh eyes.

Trick #28: Heartbeat...heartbeat...heart

Trick #29: Check the views, not the comments.

Trick #30: #Wordsaresearchable

Trick #31: Don't wait for the Academy Awards to thank your friends and family.

ABOUT THE AUTHOR

Danny Tieger is a teacher, filmmaker, singer/songwriter, actor, and a full-time creative guy. Danny has created lots of silly work for Dreamworks TV, Discovery Kids, and Story Pirates. He is also the author of *I Am Your Songwriting Journal*. He lives with his family in Connecticut.

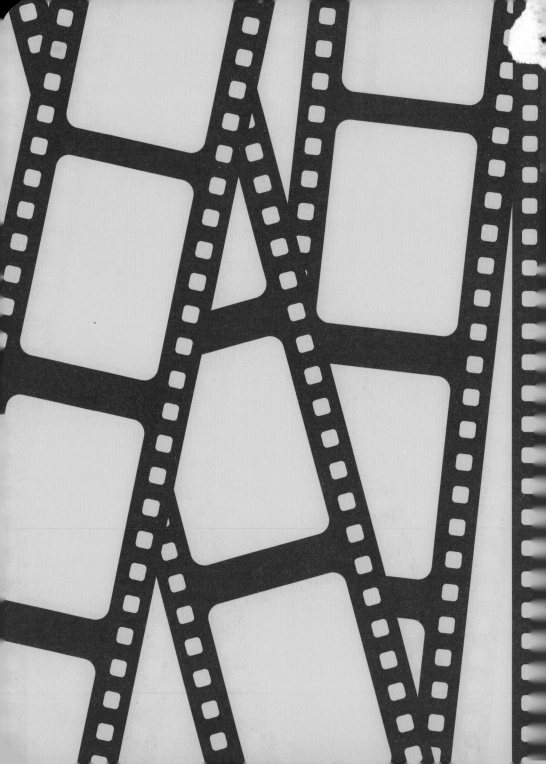